THE GOSPEL DAY BY DAY
THROUGH EASTER

The Gospel day by day through Easter

Gospel Reflections for the Easter Season

BRIAN MOORE SJ

 THE LITURGICAL PRESS
Collegeville, Minnesota

Cover by Fred Petters

Copyright © 1989 by Brian Moore. All rights reserved. First published in 1990 by St. Paul Publications, Homebush, New South Wales, Australia. This edition for the United States of America and Canada published by The Liturgical Press, Collegeville, Minnesota.

Printed in the United States of America.

1	2	3	4	5	6	7	8	9

Library of Congress Cataloging-in-Publication Data

Moore, Brian A.
    The Gospel day by day through Easter : Gospel reflections for the Easter season / Brian Moore.
        p. cm.
    ISBN 0-8146-2003-5
    1. Eastertide—Prayer-books and devotions—English.   2. Bible.
N.T. Gospels—Meditations.   3. Catholic Church—Prayer-books and devotions—English.   I. Title.
BX2170.E25M66   1991   91-7115
242'.36—dc20   CIP

Contents

Foreword

This book is offered in the hope that it may provide assistance to those who desire to live their lives in harmony with the spirit of the various Seasons of the Church's Liturgical Year.

One way in which this may be attempted is, as Vatican II says, by a 'closer attention to the word of God' — an attentiveness of mind and heart which may lead to 'more ardent prayer'.

Through the Readings appointed for each day's Liturgy of the Word we come in contact with those passages which are seen best to illuminate the spirit of each successive stage of each Season and to suggest the kind of influence it should have in our daily lives.

Not all passages of the Scriptures, however, are equally accessible in this respect. The treasure is there, but it is, in varying degrees, hidden; and we all have to unearth it for ourselves.

The following pages, it is hoped, may help.

First Week of Easter

Easter Sunday

The gospel Reading for Easter Sunday morning is normally John's account of Mary Magdalen's telling Peter and John that the tomb is empty and of the Apostles' running to see for themselves.

Alternative gospel Readings are provided for Years B and C, but since they do not recount the Easter event they are purely optional and rarely used.

The gospel Reading from the Easter Vigil (in turn Matthew, Mark and Luke) may be used in place of the Reading given for today.

In the afternoon or evening of Easter Sunday, the gospel for the Third Sunday, Year A (Luke 24:13-35 — the disciples at Emmaus) is a further option.

Easter Sunday
Years A, B, C
John 20:1-9

For all that their accounts vary, each one of the four gospel narratives of the events of the first Easter morning directs our gaze to the same focal point — an empty tomb.

Today, we have come in spirit to the tomb of Jesus — either with the holy women, with slow, sad footsteps, or running alongside of slow Peter or fleeter John; and we have seen what all of them saw, have seen all there was to see — an empty tomb.

If it is with Peter and John that we have come to the tomb, we will, hopefully, be like John, who says of himself that 'he went in, he saw, and he believed' (v. 8). If it is with the holy women that we have come, then we, too, will hear the angels' asking (playfully, I think, rather than portentiously), 'Why are you looking among the dead for someone who is alive?' (Lk 24:5).

And, perhaps, before the day is out, we shall, as did the holy women and the disciples, see Jesus standing before us, or appearing among us, saying, 'Do not be afraid; it is I — the First and the Last. I am the living one. I was dead, and now I am to live for ever and ever' (Rev 1:18).

Jesus lives; and yet, in his returning to life, there was a death — the death of Death itself. In a brief, pithy dialogue, St Augustine writes: 'Where is Death? Seek it in Christ. It is not there. It was there; but there it died. O Life, the death of Death!'

Augustine is dramatising Isaiah's prophecy, 'He will destroy death for ever' (25:48), and Hosea's taunt, 'Where is your sting, O Death?' (Hos 13:14). Jesus, rising from the dead, fulfills Isaiah's prophecy, vindicates Hosea's taunt.

But not only Jesus; we, also, *in* Jesus (in whose death and resurrection we have become sharers through baptism) fulfil the prophecy and vindicate the justness of the taunt. So St Paul writes, 'When this our mortal nature has put on immortality, then the words of the scripture will come true: Death is

11

swallowed up in victory! Death, where is your victory? Death, where is your sting?' (1 Cor 15:54).

In other words, the empty tomb which we contemplate today is our own grave already emptied of ourselves — not yet in fact, but in the certitude of a hope that cannot be disappointed. For our hope is not a holding of the breath, a crossing of the fingers. Our hope *is* Jesus, dead and risen.

Bodily death is, so to speak, the 'sacrament' of sin: it is the *sign* that sin has entered the world, the sign of the 'death' of the soul through the loss of the divine life which God willed it to have and to live by; and death is also the *seal* which would make permanent sinful man's separation from God. But in the sinless Jesus, death is the sign of others' sin: it is *our* iniquity that he has borne.

When, therefore, Jesus takes upon himself the sign of sin, death, and triumphs over it in his resurrection, he triumphs over sin itself; and his resurrection, in which we share as members of our Head, is, so to speak, the sacrament, the sign and seal of life-restored, of our reunion with God.

As far as our day to day living is concerned, the practical conclusion of our meditation on this day's great mystery is what St Paul says: 'If you have risen with Christ, seek the things that are above, where Christ sits at the right hand of God. Let your thoughts dwell on what things are in heaven, not those that are on earth. For you have died, and your life is hidden in Christ with God' (Col 3:1-3).

First Week
Monday
Matthew 28:8-15

Today's Reading presents us with two contrasting pictures — each vividly realised and easily imagined. That Matthew intends the contrast to be one of high drama is seen in the connecting clause, 'While they (Group 1) were on their way, some of the guards (introducing Group 2) went off . . .' (v. 11).

The first group portrait is a picture of belief; the second, of unbelief. And in imaginatively making ourselves participants in each group in turn, we breathe two quite different atmospheres.

In the first, we experience 'awe and great joy' (v. 8) and intimate contact with Jesus (v. 9) as we hear his friendly, 'Greetings !' (v. 9) and his reassuring, 'Do not be afraid' (v. 10). In the second, we enter into an atmosphere of hostility, agitation, corruption and deceit.

For a time, then, let us imagine ourselves a part of each scene, and savour the different feelings to which such participation gives rise, before going on to attend to the words that are spoken.

In each case, the principals give a commission which the various participants gladly accept. 'Go tell my brothers . . . ,' says Jesus. 'You must say,' the chief priests command, 'His disciples stole him away . . .'.

We pray that we accept Jesus' commission to us in our own place and time to proclaim his resurrection with full confidence in the joy the truth of it brings.

First Week
Tuesday
John 20:11-18

Like the chosen three on Mt Tabor (cf. Mt 17:1-8), like those who witnessed the Ascension of Jesus (cf. Acts 1:9-11), Mary Magdalen has gently to be told that this moment of intense tenderness and joy can not, at present, be unending.

Between any experience of Christ in faith and its fulfilment in face-to-face vision when he comes again, there lies, for every

13

one of us, a lifetime of witness — of 'going and telling' to our own world of place and time, and in our own way, the joyful news of Jesus' resurrection, and of his return to his Father who is also our Father (v. 17).

In this scene, as a Kempis notes, Mary illustrates that, 'Love knows no rest until it finds what it seeks, possesses what it loves, and gains what it desires'. But finding, gaining, possessing — all are by way of faith. Mary does not recognise Jesus when she sees him (v. 14); but she knows him in the one word he speaks (v. 16) when he says, 'Mary': for each of those who belong to him he calls personally, intimately by name (cf. Jn 10:3).

(Lord ... say but the word ... — so that I, too may say,
    Methought I heard one calling, *Child!*
    And I replied, *My Lord!*)

But Jesus, while he calls us all to intimacy, also calls us to proclamation. And so today's Reading, while it began with, 'Meanwhile, Mary stayed', ends with, 'So Mary of Magdala went'.

First Week
Wednesday
Luke 24:13-35

The Gospel Reading for today is that of the Third Sunday, Year A.

First Week
Thursday
Luke 24:35-38

The Gospel Reading for today is that of the Third Sunday, Year B.

14

First Week
Friday
John 21:1-14

The Gospel Reading for today is that of the Third Sunday, Year C.

First Week
Saturday
Mark 16:9-15*

Today, we find ourselves seated at table with the Eleven. What joy when Jesus suddenly appears among us; what consternation when he begins upbraiding his Apostles for their 'incredulity and obstinacy' (v. 14). Jesus is surely being too hard on them.

It has been suggested that the author, in view of the universal commission of proclaiming the Good News which Jesus is about to give his Church (v. 15) wishes to emphasise that the progress of that proclamation will be all God's doing — and will be achieved in the face of human unbelief and opposition.

This commission to 'proclaim the Good News to all creation', therefore, is not futile, for the Lord himself will be working with those who proclaim him (cf. Mk 16:20), will be with them until the end of time (cf. Mt 28:20).

As members of the Church we share in this commission given to the Church: '. . . the Christian vocation is, of its nature, a

---

* It is agreed that v. 8 concludes Mark's own words. Vs. 9-20 comprise the additional ending (there are others) which the Church has accepted as canonical.

vocation to the apostolate as well' (Vat II). This 'noble obligation' (Vat II) is undertaken not only through the witness of our lives (cf. Mt 5:16) but also in our actively 'contributing our share of the work for the truth' (3 Jn 8).

And as we pray that the Church will be persevering in fulfilling its obligation in the face of all human resistance, so must we pray the same for ourselves. But such prayer we make with full confidence and trust in the abiding presence of Christ to us.

Second Week of Easter

Second Sunday of Easter

The gospel Reading for this Sunday is always the same. It recounts Jesus' appearing to his disciples on Easter Sunday evening, and his coming among them again eight days later.

The doubt of Thomas and his subsequent confession of faith are situated in this Reading and bridge the interval between the two appearances of Jesus.

Second Sunday
Years A, B, C
John 20:19-31

The gospel Reading proposed for today is the conclusion to John's Gospel. (The final brief chapter appears to be something of an afterthought — a beautiful afterthought, however, containing that lovely early-morning scene of Jesus preparing breakfast for his apostles on the shore of the lake.)

The concluding verse, 'that you may believe that Jesus is the Christ and, believing this, have life through his name,' summarises John's whole purpose in writing his Gospel. It also indicates why the final incident John chooses to narrate is the coming of Thomas from a refusal to believe to making that great act of faith, 'My Lord and my God!'

There are probably many reasons one could propose to explain Thomas's refusal to believe. We get the best explanation, I think, if we recall an earlier incident involving Thomas. In John 11, we have the story of the raising of Lazarus. At the time of Lazarus' death, Jesus was on the far side of the Jordan. 'Let us go to Judea,' he says. The apostles protest that to do so would be to court danger. Thomas says, 'Let us also go — and die with him'. Thomas's love for Jesus taught him that it is better to die with Jesus than to live without him.

When, therefore, his fellow apostles tell Thomas that they have seen the Lord he refuses to believe them. To believe would be to have his heart raised high in hope and joy — only, perhaps, to have that hope dashed and that joy turned into bitterest grief should the apostles prove to have been deceived.

The very promptness with which Thomas lays down the conditions of his believing (that he himself touch the wounds in Jesus' body) speaks eloquently of how deeply those wounds were engraved in his heart and mind.

Knowing Thomas's love, Jesus is gentle with him, not reproaching him as he did others for their disbelief (cf. Mk 16:14), but inviting him to the intimacy of touching his wounded side — in which wound resides the healing of all doubts.

But it is we, not Thomas, that Jesus pronounces especially blessed: 'Happy are they who have not seen and yet believe'; and these words, taken to our hearts, provide us with encouragement in any trial, as we, too, find a refuge in the opened side of Jesus.

To believe in Jesus, to confess that 'Jesus is Lord', is possible only through the Holy Spirit who lives in us (cf. 1 Cor 12:3); and, in today's Reading, John situates the giving of the Holy Spirit in a context of coming to, or being confirmed in, faith.

The Holy Spirit is the first gift of the risen Jesus to his Church. His action of 'breathing' recalls how, in the beginning of creation, God breathed into the nostrils of the man he had fashioned, and thus man became a living being (cf. Gen 2:7).

The Holy Spirit is meant to be the breath of our daily lives — for the gift of the Spirit is meant to empower us in our mission of daily witness to Jesus. Hence, in this scene, Jesus first gives his Church its mission: 'As the Father sent me, so I am sending you'. Only then does he breathe on the Church his all-empowering Spirit.

Second Week
Monday
John 3:1-8

The Readings for the first few days of this week divide among themselves John's account of the meeting by night between Jesus and Nicodemus. The scene may be easily imagined: the two are seated opposite one another (on the floor or at table) talking, while a solitary oil-lamp illuminates their faces. The face of the younger man is kindly, confidently serene — for he knows the authority with which he speaks; that of the older man reflects good-will and, also, puzzlement. We, too, sit — out of the circle of light, but within ear-shot.

Jesus takes his cue from the sighing of the evening breeze, and uses it as an image of the working of the Spirit who is to be the first gift which he, crucified and risen, will give to his Church.

The coming and going of the wind, its cadences and crescendos, are real — if mysterious (v. 8). So it is with the action of the Spirit in the lives of those to whom it has been given. They who are children of God, says St Paul, are led by the Spirit of God (cf. Rom 8:14).

The wind, Jesus says, is supremely free (v. 8). Our freedom as children of God (cf. Rom 8:21) is directly proportioned to our docility to the Spirit who lives and works in us (cf. Rom 8:9).

Second Week
Tuesday
John 3:7-15

Today's Reading sets the same scene as yesterday's, and so we are invited to insert outselves into it, and to savour its special atmosphere, as we did then. The Reading also deliberately overlaps yesterday's to again give us Jesus' comparison between the free-blowing wind and the action of the Holy Spirit — to give us, as it did Nicodemus, something to wrestle with.

Perhaps what is puzzling Nicodemus is Jesus' insistence that he, Nicodemus, someone born of Abraham and, thereby, one of God's elect, must be 'born again'. Returning to this question of re-birth, Nicodemus abandons the quite materialistic line he took in yesterday's Reading (in v. 4) and simply, humbly, asks for enlightenment (v. 9).

21

In reply, Jesus virtually says that, for now, Nicodemus must simply believe in Jesus. Here Nicodemus (as we, too, so often are) is in a position similar to Peter's at the washing of the feet at the Last Supper when Jesus says, 'You will understand later' (cf. Jn 13:6-7).

What this passage of Scripture is saying to us, therefore, may be that we will understand the events of our own lives — exterior or interior, and the inter-play of them — only to the extent that, with complete faith in Jesus, we enter into the mystery of his (and our) passion and resurrection.

Second Week
Wednesday
John 3:16-21

Yesterday's Reading ended with Jesus' prophecy of his crucifixion (vs. 13-14); today's is taken up with John's four-fold reflection on the meaning of that death.

The crucifixion and resurrection of Jesus is the supreme proof of God's love for his creation — the measure in which he so loved the world (v. 16), and the measure, also, of Jesus' personal love for me: 'He loved *me* and delivered himself up for *me*' (cf. Gal 2:20).

The lifting up of Jesus in death is the source of eternal life for all who believe in him (v. 16); it manifests the reason for the coming of the Son into the world — not to condemn but, through self-sacrifice, to save (v. 17).

The rest of the Reading expresses John's wrestling to understand how such a demonstration of love, how such an invitation to life, could be rejected by so many who refuse 'to believe in the name (the person, the words, the works, the demonstrated love) of God's only Son' (v. 18).

That is the great mystery of human freedom; and yet acceptance or rejection of the one who was lifted up as 'a banner for all the nations' (cf. Is 49:22) is the ultimate divider of the human family (vs. 20-21) — as, long before, Simeon had foretold (cf. Lk 2:34).

As did Jeremiah (cf. 8:15) we look for — and pray for — 'a time of healing' for our human race and our own divided hearts.

Second Week
Thursday
John 3:31-36

Today's Reading gives us the Evangelist's reflection on John the Baptist's final witness to Jesus as narrated in John 3:22-28. However, the centre of attention is not the Baptist but Jesus — not the friend of the Bridegroom but the Bridegroom himself (v. 29), not the one who must decrease but the One who must increase (v. 30).

The chief concern of the passage is to contrast the one who is 'from above' and the one who is 'of the earth'; it thereby recalls Jesus' conversation with Nicodemus which constituted the Readings of the week up until now. Specifically, the two being contrasted are Jesus and John the Baptist; but more generally it is their respective baptisms and the recipients of those baptisms who are compared.

As Jesus is 'from above' so those who have faith in him and are baptised in his name are re-born from above (cf. Jn 3:3 — *Monday*). Through baptism, they have entered into the Paschal Mystery of the death and resurrection of Jesus (cf. Rom 6:3-4) and, having risen with Jesus, now 'look for the things that are in heaven where Christ is' (cf. Col 3:1) and set their minds 'on heavenly things, not on the things of earth' (cf. Col 3:2).

Baptised into Christ, they have clothed themselves in Christ (cf. Gal 2:20), are co-heirs with him in eternal life (v. 36) and are graced with the gift of the Spirit of Christ.

Eastertide is assuredly a time of joy and thanksgiving.

Second Week
Friday
John 6:1-15

The Readings for the next eight weekdays put before us the whole of the sixth chapter of John's gospel, except for the last two verses which foretell the betrayal of Jesus by Judas Iscariot — which is hardly relevant to the present season — and vs. 41-43 regarding the supposition that Jesus was the son of Joseph.

The chapter as a whole, however, is relevant — for it is mostly taken up with Jesus' discourse on the Bread of Life; and the Eucharist is the abiding memorial, and its celebration the renewal, of the Paschal Mystery of the passion and resurrection of our Lord.

'O sacred Banquet, in which Christ is received,
   the memory of his passion is recalled,
     the mind is filled with grace,
and a pledge of future glory is given us.'

Today, we begin with the miracle of the loaves and fishes, the feeding of the five thousand. Among so many people, we can, easily, sit down unchallenged with the rest, observe the miracle take place, discuss it with those around us, and, hopefully, really desire Jesus to be King over us.

The young lad, proudly if briefly the centre of attention, teaches us something very important. If he had kept for himself the little food he had, he would have satisfied his own hunger — but no one else's. But surrendered into the hands of Jesus his little feeds thousands.

24

So it is with us. What we have to offer — little or much — does not matter. What matters is our total surrender of it into the hands of Jesus for him to do with it as he will.

Second Week
Saturday
John 6:16-21

Especially if we are not good sailors, we may not enjoy putting ourselves in the boat with the disciples, and with them face the growing darkness, the rising wind, the roughening sea, and share their fears. But unless we do, we shall not hear Jesus' words, 'It is I. Do not be afraid' (v. 20) nor come to the place we are making for (v. 21).

The miracle is also a parable of our life: it is only the presence of Jesus in our lives which holds us steady; and it is only through him, and with him, and in him that we can come to the place we are, throughout our lifetime, making for. Lines of a song from *Porgy and Bess* come to mind:

Jesus is walking on the water.
Rise up, and follow him home.

Like the disciples, we are in darkness (in this Reading, a symbol of their bewilderment) until Jesus comes to us (cf. v. 17) — not through sight of him but through our hearing his Word; and as 'the disciples wanted to take him into the boat' (v. 21) so also we must be sincere in wanting him to come into our lives.

Just as this incident is both miracle and parable, so our receiving the Eucharist, wonderful reality that it is (cf. yesterday's Reading), is also symbolic of our desire to have Jesus come into and rule our lives (cf. yesterday's Reading).

Third Week of Easter

Third Sunday of Easter

In Year A, the gospel Reading relates how Jesus joins himself to two of his disciples on their way to Emmaus where he reveals himself to them in the breaking of the bread. Year B takes up his story with the immediate return of the disciples to Jerusalem.

Year C's Reading is unconnected with these events. That year's Reading is the postcript to John's Gospel which recounts Jesus' early morning meeting with some of the Apostles at the lakeside, and his foretelling of Peter's role in the Church and the death by which he would glorify God.

Third Sunday
Year A
Luke 24:13-35

It will be remembered that, on Easter Sunday morning, when Mary Magdalen sat weeping by the empty tomb and Jesus came to her, she did not recognise him until he spoke to her, calling her by name — as he does each of the stars (Ps 146[146-7]:4) and each of his sheep (Jn 10:4).

Similarly, in today's story something prevented the disciples from recognising Jesus, even though, as he explained the Scriptures to them, their hearts were set on fire. It was only when Jesus 'took bread, said the blessing, broke it, and handed it to them' that 'their eyes were opened, and they recognised him'.

What the gospel is telling us is that, after his resurrection, the presence of Jesus in the world would be recognised not through meeting him in the flesh, but through encountering him in Word and Sacrament, particularly in the Eucharist. For us, this speaks of the necessity of our hearing his word — as preached to us, or through reflection on the Scriptures — and of our frequenting the Eucharist. For the Church, it means that 'in season and out of season' (2 Tim 4:1) she must never cease from breaking for the People the bread taken from the two tables of the Word and the Eucharist. And part of our prayer should be that the Church do this constantly and, in the power of the Spirit, effectively.

'When they drew near to the village ... Jesus made as if to go on.' Jesus was not play-acting. He would certainly have gone on had not the disciples 'pressed him to stay with them' — urged to do so by their eagerness to hear him continue to speak of the One about whom they could not hear enough, and by the courtesies of hospitality.

Jesus is not pushy. In *Revelation* (3:20) he is represented as saying, 'Behold, I stand at the door and knock', adding that

29

he will enter and sit side by side and eat with anyone who will open the door to him.

There is a well-known painting by the Blessed Angelico which portrays the two disciples quite physically constraining Jesus to enter their house. The two disciples, however, are dressed in the religious habit of the Friars. It is not Angelico's whimsey which dictates this detail. He is making the important point that, in contemplating a scene from the Scriptures, it is very helpful to put ourselves into the scene either as a participant or observer.

So à Kempis writes: 'Would that I had been there and walked secretly with Jesus, by his side or behind him, attentively listening to everything my Lord and Saviour said, and carefully storing in my heart everything that I heard in order often to meditate on it afterwards. Then would I have had help to go heavenwards.'

One word of Jesus which should be ever in our mind is his saying, 'Whatever you did or did not do to even the least of those who are mine, you did or neglected to do to me' (cf. Mt 25:31-46). So often in our lives Jesus comes to us in the person of someone in need. If we do not accustom ourselves to seeing Jesus in others, then, on those occasions of his coming to us, our eyes, too, will be held and we will not recognise him, will not hear his voice, will not hear him knocking.

Third Sunday
Year B
Luke 24:35-48

The disciples mentioned in the opening words of today's Reading are the two to whom Jesus joined himself on the road to Emmaus, whose house he entered, and to whom he revealed himself in the breaking of the bread. (Cf. Year A.) At once, they hurry back to Jerusalem to tell their news; but entering the upper room they are greeted with the chorus, 'The Lord has risen, indeed, and has appeared to Simon' (cf. Lk 24:33-35). Undeterred, however, they tell their story.

'Where two or three are gathered in my name,' Jesus had said (Mt 18:20), 'there am I in the midst of them'. If ever there was a gathering together in the name of Jesus, it is this — pictured for us today by Luke. And we should find a seat for ourselves among them (for, having received the faith from them, we are already one with them in heart and mind) so that with them we, too, may see, hear, be lost in wonder, rejoice — for Jesus is suddenly visible in our midst.

The appearances of Jesus after his resurrection are characterised by this suddenness of coming and equal suddenness of departure. Little wonder, therefore, that the disciples thought that they were seeing a ghost — until they learnt that what this suddenness of coming and going meant was that their risen Lord was no longer subject to the constraints of time and place. At the same time, however, the physical reality of him is emphasised: the marks of his crucifixion are shown them; they are invited to touch him; he eats in their presence.

But more than those things, it is the witness of the scriptures which attests the reality of the resurrection of Jesus. 'So you see how it is written that the Christ would suffer and on the third day rise from the dead' (v. 46), says Jesus. So, too, in Thessalonika, 'Paul . . . for three consecutive sabbaths developed the arguments from scripture for them, explaining and proving how it was ordained that the Christ should suffer and rise from the dead' (cf. Acts 17:1-4). Again, in writing to the people at Corinth, Paul insists, 'Christ died for our sins, in accordance with the scriptures . . . and he was raised to life on the third day, in accordance with the scriptures' (cf. 1 Cor 15:3-5). And still today that is the faith we profess in the Creed: 'On the third day he rose again, in fulfilment of the scriptures' — a profession of faith we are enabled to make because the risen Jesus himself first 'opened their minds (and, through them, ours also) to understand the scriptures' (v. 45).

Having enlightened, Jesus next commissions — both the disciples and us: 'You are witnesses'. We are links in the unbroken chain of testimony to Jesus and to the purpose of his coming among men: 'that, in his name, repentance for the forgiveness of sins would be preached to all the nations' (v. 47). That testimony the Old Testament handed on to the disciples who have handed it on to us, making it our duty and our glory to hand it on to those who will come after us.

And when Jesus comes again, we shall see how strong, or how weak, a link we have been in that mighty tradition, depending on how clearly our lives, our words, our actions, our values will be shown to have been in harmony with our belief that Jesus, by dying, destroyed our death, and, by rising, restored us to life.

Third Sunday
Year C
John 21:1-19 (or 21:1-14)

It is not hard to visualise the scene in today's Reading and to savour the stillness and freshness of a lake-side at day-break; but we might do more, and enter into the scene more actively — perhaps joining the disciples in their boat and sharing their labour and experiencing the bitter taste of their disappointment; or, perhaps, remaining on the shore and gathering the driftwood which Jesus will need to make his fire.

The story cannot fail to bring to mind that other occasion involving another miraculous draught of fishes (Lk 5:1-11) when Jesus, having finished preaching from Peter's boat, tells the disciples to put out further from the shore and pay out their nets for a catch. Both then and in today's incident the story is the same: they have laboured all night and have caught nothing: but, doing as Jesus says, a great haul is taken. Each occasion is a dramatisation of Jesus' own words, 'Without me you can do nothing' (Jn 15:5).

Certainly, neither his disciples nor we, to the extent that we are all in some way 'fishers of men', will labour successfully for Jesus without the twofold acknowledgement that without them we can do nothing, but that in him we can do all things (cf. Phil 4:13). Mark concludes his Gospel (16:20) by saying that when the Apostles went out and preached everywhere, 'the Lord worked with them', confirming their words by signs. So we, too, never work alone.

Peter's reactions on these two occasions are very different. On the earlier occasion, he had fallen at Jesus' knees and said, 'Leave me, Lord; I am a sinful man' — for he recognised in Jesus something more than mortal. Here, when John recognises and identifies Jesus, saying, 'It is the Lord', Peter gathers his clothes around him and leaps into the water, in order the quicker to come to his dear Lord. Seeing his action should inspire us to pray that we at least desire to have a spark of such a love in our own hearts.

It is regarding his love that Jesus questions Peter so pressingly, compelling Peter to look deep within himself. Jesus' first formulation of his question reminds Peter of his former claim that, 'Though all lose faith in you, I will never lose faith'. In his new-found humility, Peter, in answering, speaks only for himself.

This dialogue between Jesus and Peter does more than rehabilitate Peter after his three-fold denial. It is also a solemn commissioning of him in his pastoral office, and a repetition of the call, 'Follow me'.

The call had originally been given much earlier; but now it is the crucified and risen Jesus who issues the invitation — and that circumstance lays stress on that carrying of the cross, that sharing in the death of Jesus which is an essential dimension of true discipleship.

In the case of Peter, this is made very explicit in Jesus' fore-telling his martyrdom. It is, as John notes, 'a death by which Peter would give glory to God'. Death and giving glory to God are closely associated in John's Gospel. As Jesus gives glory to God supremely in accepting an obedience which brings him to the cross, so the disciples of Jesus give glory to God to the extent that they willingly share in Jesus' crucifixion.

Jesus' words are uncompromising: 'If anyone wants to be a follower of mine, let him renounce himself, and take up his cross and follow me' (Mt 16:24). We must pray constantly that we may never even desire to compromise.

Third Week
Monday
John 6:22-29

Let us join the crowd of people who come looking for Jesus — while praying that our motives for doing so (and examining ourselves in this regard) are more worthy of him (and of ourselves) than those which Jesus attributes to them (v. 26). Ignoring their question, Jesus goes to the heart — not only to the heart of the matter, but also to the hearts of those who have just blandly asked, 'Master, when did you come here?' (v. 25).

How often had his hearers already heard those words: '. . . he made you feel hunger, he fed you with manna . . . to make you understand that man does not live on bread alone . . .' (Deut 8:3). And yet still, and even after the miracle which they had witnessed only the day before (cf. 2nd Wk, Fri.), their thoughts rise no higher than a longing for the 'food that cannot last' (v. 27).

The Samaritan woman, too, had begun by interpreting Jesus' promise of 'living water' in a material sense; but she finally came to faith (cf. Jn 4:5-52). Here, however, as we shall see day by day in the rest of the chapter, Jesus' promise, his offer of imperishable food (v. 27), is carped at, challenged, misunderstood and finally, by many, rejected.

The Sower has gone out to sow his seed; but, in great part, the soil is ill-disposed to receive it. Prejudice and presumption have hardened it.

Third Week
Tuesday
John 6:30-35

Today, we find ourselves still among that great crowd — a restive lot, impatient for a 'sign' (v. 30). How quickly they had 'forgotten' the miracle of the day before — although then it was sufficient to make them want to compel Jesus to assume kingship, and was the very reason why they were back again today.

At the end of yesterday's Reading, we find Jesus asserting that if (as they had asked) they wanted to do God's will they would believe in him, since he, Jesus, was the one whom God had sent (vs. 28-29).

Now Moses, they knew, was sent by God; and he brought them bread from heaven — bread of two kinds: the Law and the Manna (v. 31). How, they ask, can Jesus prove himself to be greater than Moses that they should take notice of him (v. 30)?

To this Jesus replies that Moses was only the intermediary of God's gifts, not their source; but *now,* at this moment, through Jesus, (on whom God has set his seal) God *is offering* them a true Law and a true Bread from Heaven which those of Moses merely foreshadowed. Had not Moses himself warned the people: 'Your God will raise up a prophet like myself . . .; to him you must listen' (Deut 18:15)?

35

Jesus speaks of a bread which means life for the world. In answer, his hearers almost parody the 'Our Father': 'Sir,' they said, 'give us that bread always'.

In what spirit do I pray that petition in the Lord's Prayer?

Third Week
Wednesday
John 6:35-40

Today, let us ignore the crowd around us — even if in their restlessness they are jostling us, and their mutterings make us have to strain to catch Jesus' words. Such words! Let us hear them now as if for the first time:

> Whoever comes to me will never be hungry ... Whoever believes in me will never be thirsty ... Whoever comes to me I will not cast out ... I have come not to do my own will but the will of him who sent me ... Whoever believes in me I shall raise up on the last day.

All we have to do to receive such blessings is to 'come' to Jesus — that is, to believe in him and, believing, entrust ourselves, and all things else, to him without reserve.

'Whoever,' says Jesus, 'sees the Son and believes in him shall have eternal life' (v. 40). To see Jesus physically does not compel belief — as we are seeing demonstrated by so many of the crowd among whom we find ourselves today. But to believe in Jesus is to see him, for faith is illumination.

Ultimately, when the blind man (cf. Mk 10:51) asks Jesus, 'Lord, that I may see!' and when the sighted man prays, 'Lord, I believe. Help my unbelief!' (cf. Mk 9:24) they are praying for the same thing — faith in Jesus.

And, for our encouragement, we recall Jesus' own words: 'Blessed are they who have not seen and yet believe' (Jn 20:29; cf. 2nd Sunday).

Third Week
Thursday
John 6:44-51

The crowd around us is muttering: 'How can he be from heaven? We know his parents' (v. 42). Jesus is peremptory: 'Stop complaining to each other' (v. 43) — and resumes his discourse at the beginning of today's Reading.

Jesus has already insisted on the necessity of coming to him, seeing him, believing in him (cf. yesterday's Reading). But this cannot happen of a person's own volition. It can only happen when people are willing to be drawn when the Father draws them (v. 44). In the question of attaining to faith — salvation — eternal life, the initiative always belongs to God. We must be 'taught by God' (v. 45); merely human perceptions will not avail.

In this process, Jesus is the indispensible Mediator — for he alone has seen the Father, from whom he comes (v. 46). In Matthew (11:27), also, Jesus insists: '. . . no one knows the Son except the Father, just as no one knows the Father except the Son . . '.

Hence, Jesus insists that he is himself the bread of life: bread which is both living and life-giving. To partake of him is to receive eternal life from him — something which, assuredly, the manna in the desert (so confidently appealed to by his hearers back in verse 31 (cf. Tues. Reading) could not give (v. 49).

Then Jesus makes the statement of which the repercussions will be felt in tomorrow's Reading: the bread of life which he is offering is his own flesh, which will be offered in sacrifice for the life of the world (v. 51).

Third Week
Friday
John 6:52-59

The crowd is shocked at the final words Jesus spoke (in yesterday's Reading): '. . . the bread that I shall give is my flesh . . .' (v. 51). No mere muttering now, but violent argument (v. 52). We wonder how many of them are thinking, 'And we thought he was the Prophet Moses spoke of, and we wanted to make him King!' (cf. v. 15: Reading of Fri. Wk. 2). And perhaps they hate Jesus all the more, since his latest words have shown up the shallowness of their earlier understanding. (People are often like that.)

They do not pretend that they have misheard, or that Jesus is speaking in symbolic language. Had they done so, they would have soon been disabused when Jesus went on — adding to 'eat my flesh' the words 'drink my blood' (vs. 53, 54, 56), and insisting that his flesh is real food, his blood real drink (v. 55). By 'real' he means that his flesh and blood do what all food and drink do — nourish, give life, and satisfy the appetite.

But what his flesh and blood nourish is the spirit; the appetite they satisfy are the longings of the spirit for union with God; the life they give is not for a time but for eternity. Through the body and blood of Jesus we come to live, now and for ever, from the life of him who lives from the living Father (v. 57).

Truly, Lord Jesus, 'You have prepared a banquet for me' (Ps 23).

Third Week
Saturday
John 6:60-69

'(Jesus) taught this doctrine at Capernaum in the synagogue' (v. 59), and now the crowd has dispersed — angry, disappointed, or simply puzzled, according as they have construed Jesus' words. Now we are on the edge of a smaller group — 'his followers'; and, in the end, there will be only Jesus, the Twelve, and ourselves — to make our own confession of faith in Jesus, and pray, 'Let me never be separated from thee'.

Jesus begs his wavering followers to have faith until the outcome of his time on earth will reveal the meaning of his words. When he has 'ascended' (v. 62) first the cross and then into heaven, and when they have received the Spirit — then they will understand. 'The flesh has nothing to offer' (v. 62): human perception, even seeing and hearing a flesh and blood Jesus, is of no avail. 'Only the Spirit gives life': the spirit of man makes man a living being; only the Spirit gives the life of faith.

The circle around Jesus grows notably smaller; and we are able, if we will, to draw closer to him.

Jesus has been uncompromising with the crowd and with the company of his followers. Now he is equally uncompromising with the Twelve — and with us, for there are many ways of withdrawing, a little or a long way, from Jesus.

'Do not press me to leave you and to turn back from your company; for wherever you go, I will go; wherever you live, I will live . . .' (Ruth 1:16-17).

Fourth Week of Easter

Fourth Sunday of Easter

This Sunday is always 'Good Shepherd Sunday'. The three Years' Readings come from John 10:1-30. Much of the chapter consists of a long discourse in which Jesus speaks of himself as the only true gate of the sheepfold and the only good shepherd of the sheep — the shepherd who, by laying down his life for his sheep, leads into eternal life anyone who listens to his voice and follows him. Years A and B take in much of this discourse, with verses 19 to 26 omitted between the end of Year A's Reading and the beginning of that of Year B.

The Year C Reading, while coming from the same chapter, is part of quite a different incident. However, shorn of its beginning and end, this brief Reading is something of a summary of the Readings of Years A and B.

Fourth Sunday
Year A
John 10:1-10

In their preaching, the Apostles insist that Jesus is not only the way to the Father but is also the *only* way since he alone, in himself, brings together in unity the human and the divine — being himself both God and man, the Word made flesh.

So St Paul writes to Timothy (in 1 Tim 2:5): 'There is only one God, and there is only one Mediator between God and mankind, himself a man, Christ Jesus'. St Peter, commanded by the Sanhedrin not to preach in the name of Jesus, refused to obey — having just told them that, 'Of all the names in the world given to men, this is the only one by which we can be saved' (Acts 4:12).

The Apostles were, of course, only repeating Jesus' own claims: 'No one can come to the Father except through me' (Jn 14:6), since, as he also says (in Mt 11:27), 'No one knows the Son except the Father, just as no one knows the Father except the Son and those to whom the Son chooses to reveal him'.

This is the claim regarding himself which Jesus, under the image of a gateway, makes in today's Reading. 'I tell you most solemnly, I am the gate of the sheepfold,' he says; and repeats, 'I am the gate'.

Mediator, Saviour, Gate: they are all one — Jesus.

Because of his uniqueness as both Gate of the Sheepfold and Shepherd of the sheep of that fold, Jesus is the only source of authority and ministry within that sheepfold. Apart from him, anyone claiming authority over the sheep is 'a thief and a brigand' (v. 1) who seeks to enter the sheepfold 'only to steal and kill and destroy' (v. 10).

Way, Truth, Life: they are all one — Jesus.

So it is that, when Jesus commissions his disciples to preach the Good News, he prefaces that commissioning with the words, 'All authority in heaven and on earth has been given to me' (Mt 28:18); and in commissioning Peter in his unique role in the Church, Jesus reminds him that the lambs and the sheep he is to feed are not Peter's own but belong, always, to Jesus himself (cf. Jn 21:15-17).

The sheep, Jesus says, recognise their shepherd's voice; and they follow him as one by one he calls them by name and leads them out to pasture. His words here prompt us to recall, and meditate upon, the Lord's saying (Is 43:1), 'Do not be afraid, for I have redeemed you; I have called you by your name, you are mine'.

Truly, we are called by name — not as anonymous members of a multitude, but as individuals who are unique, uniquely known, uniquely loved.

Jesus continues by saying that when the shepherd has brought out his flock, he goes ahead of them — as the Lord went ahead of his People as he led them out of bondage in Egypt, and they follow him because they know his voice. Us, too, he calls to follow in his footsteps — in the footsteps of his passion that we may deserve to come to the glory of his resurrection. He calls us to follow in the way of his care for all.

There are, however, many things which can prevent our hearing him call: the noise of a world which is hostile to his values; the noise we make out of our own self-importance and self-seeking. Worst of all, indifference can make us deaf to his call. We need to heed the constant urging of the psalmist reminding the People that they did not always follow the Lord who led them out and went before them: 'Would that today you would hear his voice. Do not harden your hearts' (Ps 95[94]:7-8).

Fourth Sunday
Year B
John 10:11-18

When Jesus sent out the Twelve on their first missionary journey (Mt 10:1-16) as when, also, he sent out the seventy-two disciples on theirs (Lk 10:1-16) he included in his instructions to them this warning: 'Remember, I am sending you out like sheep among wolves ...' — for they were those whom he himself called his 'little flock' (Lk 12:32).

In time, they and their successors will become the shepherds of the flock of Christ; and in his own person Jesus puts before them what a good, a model, shepherd should be — in contrast with the hired man. Peter echoes his Master: 'Now I have something to say to your Elders ... Be shepherds of the flock of God that is entrusted to you: watch over it, not simply as a duty but gladly, because God wants it; not for sordid money, but because you are eager to do it' (cf. 1 Pet 5:1-2).

Similarly, Paul tells the Elders at Ephesus, 'Be on your guard for yourselves and for all the flock of which the Holy Spirit has made you overseers' ... (for) ... 'fierce wolves will invade you and will have no mercy on the flock' (cf. Acts 20:28-29).

The model shepherd, Jesus says, is characterised by two things: willingness to lay down life itself for the sheep (v. 11), and a knowledge of the sheep as intimate as the mutual knowledge which exists between himself and his Father (vs. 14-15). (Cf. Year A.) Jesus elsewhere, also, associates shepherding with dying. In Mark (14:27) he applies to himself the prophecy, 'I shall smite the shepherd, and the sheep will be scattered'; and he follows his threefold commission of his sheep to Peter's care immediately with the prophecy of Peter's martyrdom (cf. Jn 21).

Paul's warning to the Elders, to be on their guard for themselves as well as for the flock, reminds us that we are all in one respect sheep, and in some respect shepherds who have responsibility, of one kind or another, for others. And we, too, are sent out as sheep among wolves — witnesses to Christ in a world hostile to the mind of Christ, the values of Christ.

We must, therefore, watch out for ourselves and for others — but without anxiety, for, as sheep, our Shepherd is still with us to lead us; as shepherds, we have the example of Jesus to follow, and the light and strength of the Holy Spirit who has given us whatever responsibility for others we may have.

This good Shepherd of ours has already laid down his life for us, his sheep, and for those to thom we, in turn, are shepherds; and having taken that life up again, he is with us always, even, as he himself said, to the end of time (cf. Mt 28:20).

Always, he himself is still the Shepherd of all his sheep; and he continues, through us and through our active witness, to keep all his sheep under his watchful eye (cf. Ez 34:11-16), to seek out the sheep that are not yet of his fold, as well as those of his fold who have strayed.

The parable of the lost sheep (cf. Lk 15:4-7) springs readily to mind. The owner of the lost sheep, finding it, takes it joyfully on his shoulders — as willingly as Jesus did the cross by which he so dearly purchased his sheep; and, carrying what he loves and loving what he carries, he brings it back to the safety of his Father's sheepfold.

Our baptism, which we re-call in order to re-new in this Easter season, is Jesus' commission to us to join him in this his saving activity, his call to us, his sheep, to be also, in some measure, shepherds of his flock.

Fourth Sunday
Year C
John 10:27-30

The force of Jesus' words in today's Reading is better felt if they are placed in the context in which they appear in John's Gospel, and if we make ourselves active observers of the scene as well as hearers of the words. Abbreviated, the verses preceding today's Reading run: *It was winter, and Jesus was in the Temple, walking up and down in the Portico of Solomon. The Jews gathered round him and said ... 'If you are the Christ, tell us plainly'. Jesus replied, 'I have told you, but you do not believe ... because you are no sheep of mine'.*

St Augustine notes that, in asking their question, Jesus' interrogators were not seeking the truth but something to use against him — as, indeed, they found; for the verse immediately following today's few lines begins with, 'They fetched stones with which to stone him', because, they said, his words regarding his oneness with the Father were, in fact, a claim to godhead.

Augustine continues: 'It was winter, and they were cold — for they were slow to draw near to the divine fire . . .'. 'Lacking the fire of love, they were cold — and yet they were on fire with the desire to hurt. They had gone far from him — and yet they were there. They were not drawing near by believing — and yet pressed him close by attacking him.'

Elsewhere, Jesus says, 'If you love me, keep my commandments' (Jn 14:15). Here he says that faith in him is demonstrated by listening to his voice, showing thereby that we are his sheep — those whom he feeds with the word of life, and who follow him who is the Life into eternal life. Commenting on the unwillingness of Jesus' interrogators to draw near, Augustine remarks, 'To draw near is to believe; for the soul is not moved by feet but by longings'.

There is irony in the setting of this scene, an irony which intensifies the ugliness of the hardened heart which willfully misundertands everything Jesus says.

The confrontation takes place in the Portico of Solomon, a name which means 'peace' — and Jesus is, indeed, the King of Kings and Prince of Peace. He is our Peacemaker who makes peace between mankind and God through his blood shed on the cross (cf. Col 1:20); and he is the only giver of true peace (cf. Jn 14:27). Earlier, Jesus had reminded his hearers how the Queen of the South 'came from the ends of the earth to hear the wisdom of Solomon', and added, 'and there is something greater than Solomon here' — himself (Cf. Lk 11:31). But, today, his enemies come not to hear the Word and Wisdom of the Father, but only darkly to question, coldly to challenge and, finally, attempt to kill.

Solomon's other name was Jedidiah, meaning 'beloved of Yahweh'; and the Father himself had proclaimed, at Jesus' Baptism and Transfiguration, that Jesus was more than beloved of him, was, indeed, his beloved Son. Already Jesus' claim here, 'The Father and I are one', had been vindicated.

At the Transfiguration of Jesus, the Father's voice added, 'Listen to him'. To listen is to believe; to believe is to follow — to follow Jesus as sheep who follow the best of shepherds (cf. Year A).

Fourth Week
Monday
John 10:1-10

The Gospel Reading for today is that of the Fourth Sunday, Year A.

Fourth Week
Tuesday
John 10:22-30

The Gospel Reading for today is part of that of the Fourth Sunday, Year C.

Fourth Week
Wednesday
John 12:44-50

The resurrection of Jesus vindicates the claims he made during his public life — claims as to his relationship with the Father, and of his crucial significance to the human race into which he had entered in becoming man. Today's Reading is a brief statement of those claims, and, therefore, an invitation to faith on our part.

Introducing these words of Jesus, John simply says, 'Jesus declared publicly' (v. 44); he gives no context for them, sets no scene for us to visualise. We must create our own — perhaps even taking the situation out of the public arena and hearing the words in an intimate setting of just Jesus and I.

To 'see' Jesus and to 'believe' in him is to see and believe in the Father; to listen to Jesus' words is to listen to the Father from whom Jesus has the words he speaks (v. 50).

In his total fidelity and obedience to his Father, Jesus becomes a light (v. 46) which shows up for what it is the darkness of the unbelief and the refusal to listen to those who hear his words. At the same time he is a light beckoning to those who acknowledge the darkness they are in and wish to be delivered from it (v. 46). For those who refuse to listen, Jesus' words are judgement (v. 48); for those who hear and act upon them, Jesus' words are salvation (v. 50).

Jesus' words are divisive (cf. Mt 10:34-36), our response to them decisive.

Fourth Week
Thursday
John 13:16-20

The disciples to whom Jesus addresses the words of today's Reading are still dumbfounded at the fact that their Lord and Teacher has just washed their feet. What he has done, he tells them, is an example for them to copy (v. 15). Henceforth, humble service of others is to be a sign of discipleship of Jesus, a sign that a follower of Jesus has the spirit of Jesus.

'The servant is not greater than the master': the disciples are not to think that it would be beneath them to do as Jesus has done — even after he has commissioned them and sent them (as he was sent by the Father) and they have been welcomed as bearers of Good News. For the one sent is not greater than the sender; and, in this case, they are sent by Jesus as he was sent — not to be served but to be servants (cf. Mt 20:28).

Jesus gives his disciples these warnings in the context of his imminent betrayal and passion. In these respects, too, they are not greater than their Master. Their discipleship of him will invite, not render them immune from betrayal and persecution. But if they are faithful in their imitation of Jesus, happiness will be theirs (v. 17).

For us, in his passion, Jesus put aside his life (as here his outer garment). Having washed us clean, and having, in his resurrection, taken up his life again, he now addresses to us these selfsame words.

Fourth Week
Friday
John 14:1-6

As yesterday, we again find ourselves observing and listening to Jesus and his disciples gathered around the table of the Last Supper. One of them, we notice, has left the room and will never return there — or to discipleship of Jesus and fellowship with the Eleven.

The disciples are clearly upset: Jesus has spoken of betrayal and of his going from among them, and has just foretold Peter's three-fold denial. To comfort them, Jesus speaks words of reassurance: 'Do not let your hearts be troubled' (v. 1).

He assures them that his departure is for their benefit: it is only through his death that he can open for them the door of his Father's house. He further assures them that he will return to them, and that ultimately they and he will be inseparably together again. This reunion and abiding union of Jesus with his followers is achieved only through Jesus who is one with the Father — who is, therefore, 'Our Journey and our journey's End'.

'I am the Way,' Jesus says (v. 6), and because he is also the Light and the Truth and the Life, he also says, 'Anyone who follows me will not be walking in darkness, but will have the light of life' (cf. Jn 8:12).

But the way that Jesus himself took to enter into his Father's glory was the way of the Cross. Nor is there, for his followers, any other way — as he himself said: 'Anyone who wishes to be a follower of mine must take up his cross, daily, and follow me' (cf. Mt 16:24).

Fourth Week
Saturday
John 14:7-14

Today's Reading takes up where yesterday's left off, and so we are still in the Supper Room, observing Jesus and listening to him talking — at this point, chiefly of his unique relationship with his Father. To that Father he is soon to ascend, taking his place at the Father's right hand and remaining for ever to make intercession for us (cf. Heb 7:25). In this, his unceasing high priestly prayer in the heavenly liturgy we find yet another way in which Jesus is with us always.

Jesus' words today are interrupted by an interjection from Philip (v. 8) — an interjection which speaks of his deep desire for God, but which also shows how far he is from understanding Jesus' words. His request separates Father and Son, and Jesus must again explain the mutual indwelling of himself and his Father, unveiling to the eyes of faith the inmost life of the Trinity — in which life we are all meant to share.

Consequently, Jesus' words and works (the two ways in which he reveals the Father to mankind) are the words and works of his Father (vs. 10, 12), and the glorification of Jesus is to the glory of the Father (v. 13). To that Father Jesus will soon return in order to send upon his followers the Holy Spirit who will enable them also to continue Jesus' own word (v. 12).

Jesus' promise of his active cooperation with his followers (v. 14) is something on which we can wholly rely as we, too, labour in word and work for the coming of the Kingdom.

Fifth Week of Easter

Fifth Sunday of Easter

Each Year's gospel Reading is particular to that Year. Year A presents Jesus to us as the Way, the Truth and the Life. In Year B, Jesus is the Vine of whom we are the branches. In Year C, Jesus is the One who loves us and commands that we love one another in like manner.

All these gospel Readings are taken from John's narrative of Jesus' farewell discourse to his disciples at the Last Supper — Jn 13:33-16:33.

Fifth Sunday
Year A
John 14:1-12

'I am the Way, the Truth, and the Life.'

Briefly, but with power to move the heart, a Kempis (*Imitation* III. 56. 1) comments: 'Without the way, there is no going; without the truth, there is no knowing; without the life, there is no living. I am the Way which you must follow, the Truth which you must believe, the Life for which you must hope. I am the Way inviolable, the Truth infallible, the Life unending. I am the straightest Way, the sovereign Truth, the true Life, the blessed Life, the uncreated Life. If you continue in my way, you will know the truth, and the truth will make you free (cf. Jn 8:32) and you will come to life everlasting (cf. Mt 19:29).'

Jesus says of himself, 'I am the Life' (Jn 11:25) for 'what was created in him was life' (Jn 1:3); and the purpose of his coming among us was, he says, that we might have life, and have it to the full (Jn 10:10). He comes among us, therefore, in order to give himself to us. He is, therefore, both Life and the Way to life — just as he is the living and life-giving Bread.

Being the incarnate Word of the Father, Jesus is also the Truth, and the speaker of a truth which is life-giving. My words, he says, 'are spirit and they are life' (Jn 6:63); and Peter acknowledges this when he says 'Lord, to whom shall we go? You have the words of eternal life (Jn 6:68).' Again, Jesus says, 'Whoever listens to my words and believes in the one who sent me has eternal life . . . has passed from death to life' (Jn 5:24); and he urges us to make our home in his word in order to come to the truth that will make us free (cf. Jn 8:31-32).

'No one,' says Jesus, 'knows the Father except the Son' (Mt 11:27); and so, 'no one comes to the Father except through me' (Jn 14:6). Jesus is, therefore, not only the Way to the Father, but the only way (cf. 4th Sunday, Year A); and, being one with the Father, he is both our Journey and our journey's End. The following of him, therefore, is unique among journeys; for not only is he the Way in which we must go, he is also himself the most desired Goal of our going.

We follow Jesus when we believe; we possess the Truth when we believe; we have life to the extent that we believe in Jesus. For he is the Beginning and Consummation of our faith (cf. Heb 12:2); to see him (and 'we walk by faith and not by sight': 2 Cor 5:7) is to see the Father who sent him — as he tells Philip in today's Reading; to know him is to have eternal life (Jn 17:3); to believe in him is to possess already that life which, although at present hidden with him in God, is already glorious with the glory that will be revealed in us when he comes again (cf. Col 3:2-4).

What follows? — that we should love him, and adhere to him through the Spirit who has been given us (cf. Rom 5:5), and given for no other purpose than to draw us to him through whom we have access to the Father, from whom comes all life, through the Son, by the working of the Holy Spirit, and who, from age to age, through the Holy Spirit, gathers in unity in Christ a people whom he calls his own (cf. Third Eucharistic Prayer).

Fifth Sunday
Year B
John 15:1-8

'There was a vine; you uprooted it from Egypt. To plant it, you drove out other nations; you cleared a space where it could grow . . .' (Ps 80[79]:8-9).

And again, 'Let me sing to my friend the song of his love for his vineyard' (cf. Is 5:1-7). In the Old Testament, both vine and vineyard represent Israel; and in 'The Song of the Vineyard' Isaiah describes in detail how God, as Vinedresser, did everything necessary to protect and cultivate it; so much so that he could issue the challenge, 'What could I have done for my vineyard that I have not done?' Yet he vowed, 'I will lay it waste; for, 'I expected it to yield grapes. Why did it yield sour grapes instead?'

On the whole, Israel was faithless and fruitless, and failed to fulfil God's expectations. In his parable of the wicked husbandmen (Mt 21:23-46) Jesus himself uses this lament from Isaiah, and concludes by telling his hearers 'that the Kingdom of God will be taken away from you and given to a people who will produce its fruit.'

Hence, in today's Reading, Jesus first says, 'I am the *true* vine' — just as he also says that he is the genuine shepherd (cf. 4th Sunday, all Years). In the Son's becoming man, God plants a new vine in his creation — Jesus, who, by his obedience, fulfils the expectations of the Vinedresser; and when the fruit of that vine is pressed out in the winepress of the cross as the blood of the new and everlasting covenant, Jesus wins eternal redemption for all who obey him as he obeyed his Father. This is the fruitfulness of Jesus; and this fruitfulness glorifies the Father. As Jesus' sonship is manifested by his giving glory to the Father, so our discipleship of Jesus is manifested by our giving glory to the Father through our fruitfulness (v. 8).

How we are to become fruitful is explained by the vine-and-branches image which Jesus here puts before us (which, later, Paul will translate into the image of the Mystical Body of Christ) and briefly indicates three consequences that the image implies for us.

As branches of the vine, we live by the life of Christ; that is our great privilege. As branches of the vine, we must be fruitful; that is our duty. As branches of the vine, we must accept pruning, which is simply another image for what Jesus so often insists upon — that we share in his passion and cross.

To live united to Jesus, to live with the life of Jesus through his word's finding a home in us and through our making our home in his word — this is the sole, but totally necessary, condition of our being fruitful. (Cf. the role of the word of

Jesus in the two instances of a miraculous draught of fishes in the Reading for the 3rd Sunday, Year C.)

That 'word' (which is also the word which 'prunes' — or, perhaps, 'cleanses' us (cf. Jn 13:10) is generally taken to mean the 'new commandment' which Jesus gives his followers: 'Love one another as I have loved you' (cf. Jn 13:34).

Fruitfulness is the 'fruit of the vine' — not the grapes but the wine pressed from them in the winepress. Christian love (Christ's love for us and ours for one another) is eucharistic. If a single grain of wheat chooses not to be milled, it cannot become part of the bread of the Eucharist. If a single grape refuses to be pressed, it cannot become part of the wine of the Eucharist.

This is what it means to deny ourselves, as Jesus says so often we must: it means, essentially, the total commitment of our individual selves to the building up of that community which is the Body of Christ.

Fifth Sunday
Year C
John 13:31-33a, 34-35

With the departure of Judas, Jesus is left alone with those who were truly his own in the world (cf. Jn 13:1). To them he leaves the legacies of his own peace, of the example of service which he gives in his washing their feet, of his own Body and Blood. In today's Reading, he leaves them yet another legacy — a new commandment.

'Love one another,' he says; and so that there can be no doubt as to what that commandment implies, he adds, 'as I have loved you' — and we may take that *as* to be indicative of both the extent of Jesus' love and the manner of his loving.

When Jesus delivers this same commandment a second time (Jn 15:12) he adds: 'A man can have no greater love than to lay down his life for his friends' — in proof of which, 'he loved me, and delivered himself up for me' (cf. Gal 2:20). If we are to imitate the extent of the love of Jesus we, too, must be prepared 'to lay down our lives' for others. To lay down one's life does not necessarily mean literally to die, though it may; it does necessarily mean to live a life of service to others — for to do this means to die to oneself and to all self-love. It is thus that we, his pupils and his servants, grow to be like our teacher and master (cf. Mt 10:25) who came 'not to be served but to serve, and to give his life as a ransom for many' (cf. Mk 10:45).

Jesus' out-pouring of his love (and so it must be with us) did not depend on the worthiness of its recipients. On the contrary, 'it was while we were yet sinners that Christ died for us' (cf. Rom 5:8). Love must not wait on signs of lovableness before it is given.

In his own love for us, Jesus, so to speak, models himself on the first and greatest commandment: You must love God with all your heart, all your mind, and all your strength (cf. Mk 12:30). That is how he has loved us, and how we must love one another.

Jesus loved us with all his heart, that is, tenderly — with a love so tender that rather than lose me he became a man like me, became my brother in the flesh. He took upon himself my weakness in order to give me his strength, my death in order to give me his life.

So, too, our love for others must be from the heart, a true sympathy for them in their need, a genuine sharing of one another's burdens so as to fulfil the law of Christ (cf. Gal 6:2).

Jesus loved us with all his mind, that is, wisely; and in the wisdom of his love he took upon himself all the burdens of our humanity: hunger, thirst, homelessness, misunderstanding and persecution by others, betrayal by friends — and all this in order to teach us, in his own person, that nothing need come between us and God's love for us which he personifies (cf. Rom 8:38-39).

So, too, our love for others must be wise — not simply a feeling of foolish kindness which does no good to us or to anyone else. Love is wise when it seeks nothing for itself but only the true good of another.

Finally, Jesus loved us with all his strength — perseveringly, and 'to the end' (cf. Jn 13:1). Perseverence in love of others, even in the face of seeming ineffectualness or obvious rejection, is ultimately what distinguishes a love which is grounded in Christ from what is really mere self-seeking (cf. 1 Cor 13:1-13).

Fifth Week
Monday
John 14:21-26

Again we are still in the room of the Last Supper, looking at and listening to Jesus. Jesus' talk about going away from them has made his disciples uneasy. We can sense their disquiet, and feel for them.

Jesus tells them that love of him expresses itself in 'keeping his commandments, keeping his word' (vs. 21, 23) — that is to say, in shaping our lives according to his teaching, and doing so because we love him for his loving us so much as to come among us and reveal the Father to us.

'The soul,' says Catherine of Siena, 'cannot live without loving; and always unites itself with what it loves and is transformed by it'. Loving Jesus, we come to be like Jesus and, therefore, beloved of the Father (vs. 21, 23). And since love is unitive, uniting the lover and the loved, our love of Jesus brings about the divine indwelling in us (v. 23).

Those who do not love cannot 'see' Jesus. Judas' question (v. 22) is answered: it is not that Jesus withholds himself from anyone, but that disbelief cannot lead to love, revelation, or fellowship.

As for the world, it is for the Apostles and the Church whose foundation stones they are, and for the members of the Church in their own place and time, to reveal Jesus to the world through their witness to him.

Fifth Week
Tuesday
John 14:27-31

'Peace.' To the disciples gathered around him at table, Jesus speaks their people's customary word of greeting and farewell. It is an appropriate word at this moment when the disciples are disquieted at Jesus' constant talk of leaving them.

But it is more than a salutation, more than a prayer. His word is a word of power, able to bring about what it signifies. So he calmed the troubled sea: 'Peace! Be still!' he said, 'and there came a great calm' (cf. Mk 4:35-41). So, too, at Jesus' assurance, peace came to the woman who was a sinner (cf. Lk 7:36-50).

Jesus is the Prince of Peace (cf. Is 9:6), and so it is his own peace he gives us — a peace which enables us to reject anxiety by casting all our care upon him (cf. 1 Pet 5:7), to reject fear, knowing that he is with us always.

The world cannot give peace because the Prince of this world is the Prince of Darkness. With him, as a pre-requisite of his entry into the glory he had with the Father before time began (cf. Jn 17:5), Jesus must enter into mortal combat and, by dying and rising again, overcome (v. 30).

It is this above all which will make clear for all to see how the Son loves the Father — by accepting an obedience unto death, even to death on the cross (cf. Phil 2:6-11).

As Paul notes in that same place (v. 5) that has to be our mind also.

Fifth Week
Wednesday
John 15:9-11

The Gospel Reading for today is that of the Fifth Sunday, Year B.

Fifth Week
Thursday
John 15:9-11

'As the Father has loved me, so I have loved you' (v. 9). For us, the word 'as' is wonderfully ambiguous: 'Because the Father has loved, I have loved you'; and also, 'In the manner and to the degree that the Father has loved me, in that way and with that total intensity I have loved you.' The Father's love for the Son is the love which the Son has for all with whom he has become one in becoming man. How can we comprehend what it is to be loved by One who is purely Love?

'Remain in my love' (v. 9). Who would want to do otherwise? Again there is a beautiful ambiguity: 'Continue to live in and rejoice in being loved by me'; but also, 'Continue to find life and true happiness by persevering in your love for me'.

Once more Jesus reminds us that 'keeping his commandments', that is, shaping our lives according to his teaching, is the means by which we remain in his love, in both senses.

Doing so, we enjoy his joy (v. 11) — and to the full. Just as Jesus alone can give true peace (cf. Tuesday) since 'he is our peace' (cf. Eph 2:14) so he alone can give true joy — he who *is* the Joy of man's desiring. And as his peace is something which the world can not give (cf. Jn 14:27) so his joy is something which nothing can take from us (cf. Jn 16:22).

Let us rejoice and be glad.

Fifth Week
Friday
John 15:12-17

The 'commandment' of Jesus which we are to keep in order to remain one with him in friendship, and through him one with the Father, is that we love one another. Nor is the manner of our doing this left up to ourselves. Jesus is explicit: we are to love one another as he himself has loved us; and he has loved us as the Father has loved him (v. 12).

The essence of the love which Jesus is talking about is self-giving in the service of others; and he points to his own self-sacrificial death on behalf of humankind as the supreme example of such love (v. 13).

There are many ways of laying down one's life for others. Whenever we put ourselves and our selfishness aside in order to be of service to others, we are, to some extent, laying down our lives. So Jesus, who died for us, also says that he has made known to us everything he has learnt from his Father (v. 15). The life, the time, the gifts which God has given us are not meant to serve solely our own needs and desires. He gives so that we, too, are able to give.

It is in this willingness to give that we prove ourselves to be fruitful branches of the true Vine (v. 16), true imitators of Jesus, true children of our Father in heaven — of whom it is appropriate to ask only if we are willing to give (v. 17).

Fifth Week
Saturday
John 15:18-21

Jesus had said to Nicodemus: '. . . everybody who does wrong hates the light and avoids it for fear his actions should be exposed . . .' (cf. Jn 3:20); and the truth of these words will be demonstrated supremely in the way in which the Light of the world is treated by the world.

'A servant is not greater than his master' (v. 19), and the world which tried to extinguish *the* Light will similarly try to extinguish those who have taken something of that Light.

Jesus had already warned his followers of this: 'You will be hated by all men on account of my name . . .' (cf. Mk 13:13); 'You will be dragged before governors and kings for my sake . . .' (cf. Mt 10:18 — where Jesus adds the providential reason for the persecution of his followers: '. . . to bear witness before them . . .').

Like 'laying down one's life' (cf. Friday) suffering persecution can range from martyrdom to petty discrimination or mockery. What we suffer is not as important as the spirit in which we accept it (as the Spirit will enable us to do) — ultimately because in some way, small or great, it makes us that much more like Jesus our Master.

'They will do all this,' says Jesus, 'because they do not know the One who sent me' (v. 21). Our expectation of or experience of persecution is not to cause us to withhold understanding, and the compassion which springs from it. Ours must be the prayer of Jesus: 'Father, forgive them. They know not what they do' (cf. Lk 23:34).

Sixth Week of Easter

Sixth Sunday of Easter

The gospel Reading for each Year is particular to that Year, but each of them comes from Jesus' farewell discourse to his disciples at the Last Supper — Jn 13:33-16:33.

Years A and C include a promise of the gift of the Holy Spirit, while Year B again returns to the commandment to love one another as Jesus has loved us, and includes Jesus' bequeathing us his peace and naming us 'friends'.

*The Thursday of the Sixth Week is the usual day for celebrating **The Ascension of the Lord**. In some places, however, it is celebrated on the Seventh Sunday of Easter. Where this is so, the Thursday of the Sixth Week becomes an ordinary Easter weekday with its proper Readings. The celebration of the Ascension suppresses the Sunday if it is transferred to that day.*

In the pages that follow, allowance has been made for this variation by the provision of a reflection on the Gospel Readings appointed for the Thursday of the Sixth Week and the Seventh Sunday, as well as a reflection on the Ascension itself.

Sixth Sunday
Year A
John 14:15-21

To us, chronologically minded as we are, today's Reading can be a bit puzzling. In verse 16, Jesus says that he will ask the Father to send the Holy Spirit upon the disciples; then in verse 17, he tells the disciples that the Spirit is *with* them and *in* them.

John does not think of the passion and death of Jesus, his resurrection and ascension, the giving of the Holy Spirit and the Spirit's consequent indwelling of those who receive him as a chain of events, but as a single reality — and, moreover, a reality which totally transcends the space-time dimension in which all things exist and by which our thinking is conditioned.

Earlier (Jn 7:37-39) when Jesus cried out that streams of living water would flow from the breast of whoever believed in him, John added the explanation, 'As yet the Spirit had not been given because Jesus had not yet been glorified.' The 'glorification' of Jesus is, for John, his crucifixion. It is Jesus' being 'lifted up' (cf. Jn 3:14; 8:28; 12:34); but this being 'lifted up' is not only in death on the cross in the sight of the people but also into glory at the right hand of the Father in the sight of all creation. For the crucifixion of Jesus is already luminous with the light of the resurrection — that supreme sign of the Father's favour; and it is in the moment of death that Jesus 'yields up the Spirit'.

It is the reality which matters, not the chronology; so much so that in the moment of Judas' leaving the supper room in order to complete his betrayal, Jesus exults, saying, '*Now* is the Son of Man glorified' (Jn 13:31). That is to say, with Judas' going, a definitive beginning has been made to the chain of events which will culminate in the coming of the Holy Spirit. What has yet to happen in time is already accomplished in its spiritual reality.

We may find it difficult to share John's vision, but we can easily, and with profit, adapt it to our own lives. We know that the Spirit is with us (by his constantly moving us to desire to do good and avoid evil) and is in us (by his in-dwelling us through grace); but we also know that his being with us and in us can constantly be 'increased' — that is to say, intensified and made more operative, as, with ever-growing desire, we pray, 'Come, Holy Spirit'.

As St Hilary says, 'The Gift (that is, the Holy Spirit) is one, yet is offered, and offered fully, to all. Always available, it is given in proportion to each one's will to receive. It remains with each according to each one's will to grow in merit.'

When dawn breaks, we can rejoice in the gift of daylight; but, even so, it would be odd not to look forward to, to desire, the brightness of full day. Even if we do not, the daylight will inexorably grow.

However, that is not the case with the presence of the Holy Spirit within us and to us. We must desire it, and show the genuineness of our desire by our docility to his promptings and by the alacrity with which we follow his leadings. Just so, Jesus here says that we show our love for him by keeping his commandments.

Sixth Sunday
Year B
John 15:9-17

Today's Reading, towards the end, contains echoes of Jesus' words regarding the Vine and the branches, with the imperative, 'Be fruitful' (cf. 5th Sunday, Year B). However, it is Jesus' election of us to friendship with him and his commandment, 'Love one another as I have loved you', which predominate (cf. 5th Sunday, Year C).

'As the Father has loved me, so I have loved you; and as I have loved you, so you must love one another'. The words are few and simple; their implications are overwhelming: to know Jesus' love for us we need to know the Father's love for his Son; and that love, made visible in Jesus, is the standard which Jesus sets before his followers in their love for one another.

It is difficult to believe, let alone comprehend, what it means to be the receiver of the love of one who is himself simply Love (cf. 1 Jn 4:8), to believe and comprehend that we are loved by him not only because as Maker of all he is Lover of all and loves all that he has made but also simply because 'his love solicits his heart to seek ours' (St Francis de Sales). Jesus not only wants us to receive his love, he desires, also, to receive our love, given in turn.

'I have loved you with an everlasting love,' he says, 'and therefore have I drawn you' (cf. Jer 31:3) — out of nothingness into being, out of darkness into light, out of sin into grace, out of death into life, for he has drawn us to himself who is All, is Graciousness, is Light and Life.

Nor does he but protest his love; he proves it — by becoming a father to us in his creation of us, a brother to us by becoming one of us, a redeemer to us by his dying for us in fulfilment of his own words, 'No one can show greater love than to lay down his life for friendship sake' (v. 13).

He calls us not servants but friends (v. 15), and he proves his friendship of us by making known to us everything he himself learnt from his Father (v. 15) and by communicating to us his own joy (v. 11).

In every way he has loved us, those who are his own in the world (cf. Jn 13:1), and has shown how complete and without reservation his love is — even, in life, leaving himself to us as our spiritual food and drink, and, when he was dead, pouring out upon us the last drops of blood from his heart of love in order to cleanse our consciences of dead works to serve the living God (cf. Heb 9:14). And, having risen from the dead and having returned to the Father — paradoxically, in order to remain with us until the end of our own time on earth (cf. Mt 28:20) — he pours out on us his own Spirit to be our Counsellor, Comforter, Strengthener, Teacher.

How can we return such love? By living no longer for ourselves but for him who died for us and rose for us and pleads for us (cf. Eucharistic Prayer IV; Rom 8:34). And we can know that we are doing this only if we are trying to love one another as he has loved us — whole-heartedly, unselfishly, perseveringly (cf. 5th Sunday, Year C).

Sixth Sunday
Year C
John 14:23-29

In today's Reading, Jesus again promises the gift of the Holy Spirit, whom he also calls the Advocate and the Teacher of all truth (cf. Year A).

However, it is his talking of peace and of a heart untroubled and unafraid which suffuses the whole passage with an atmosphere all its own. We might do well, therefore, to begin our prayer by wordlessly savouring that atmosphere — for we, too, are there in spirit, and Jesus' words are meant for us no less than for the disciples. He wills that we, too, come to possess hearts which are untroubled and unafraid since they are filled with that peace 'which surpasses all understanding' (cf. Phil 4:7) but which may be ever more deeply experienced, savoured, and rejoiced in.

Peace springs from reconciliation; and reconciliation, if it is to be complete, is threefold. Reconciled to God, we are at peace with God; reconciled to others, we are peace with them; made whole within ourselves, we are reconciled to ourselves and are at peace. All this healing is mediated to us through Jesus, whom we rightly call 'our Peace and Reconciliation' (cf. Litany of the Sacred Heart).

It was he who reconciled us to God, 'making peace by his blood shed on the cross' (Col 1:20). Again, 'He is the peace between us' (cf. Eph 2:14) who are all so different. And if we 'keep his commandments' (v. 10) and make his will our will by 'shouldering his yoke' (cf. Mt 11:28-30) we shall find, as he promises, peace of soul. 'Blessed are the single hearted, for they shall enjoy much peace,' says the *Imitation* (I. 11); and the single heart we should desire and strive to possess is the heart which Jesus himself proposes to us to learn from — that is to say, his own (cf. Mt 11:29).

When Jesus says, 'Peace be with you', he speaks more than a word of greeting, more than a prayer. His word is a word of power, able to effect what it signifies; and so when he says, 'Peace! Be still!', there 'falls a great calm' — be it upon the troubled sea (cf. Mk 4:35-41) or the troubled human spirit (cf. Lk 7:36-50).

Jesus' words, 'My own peace I give you' give us the courage to reject anxiety by casting all our care upon him, knowing that he is looking after us (cf. 1 Pet 5:7); they give us the courage to reject fear, in the knowledge that he is always with us (cf. Mt 28:20) together with the Father (v. 23) and the Holy Spirit (v. 26); they give us courage to reject that rebellion of our own will against his will, and to experience for ourselves, 'In his will is our peace' (Dante).

The angels who heralded the coming of Jesus proclaimed 'peace on earth'; and all who welcome the coming of Jesus into their lives inherit his peace, and, in turn, bequeath it to others — thereby obtaining the blessing of seeing God which is given to the peacemakers (cf. Mt 5:9).

One of the psalms (Ps 34[33]:13-14) lays down the conditions of a happy life: 'Malice must be banished from your tongue, deceitful conversation from your lips. Never yield to evil; practise good. Seek peace, and pursue it'. This advice Peter repeats when he is describing the spirit in which a christian community should live (cf. 1 Pet 3:8-12). For the spirit in which a christian community should live is the Holy Spirit himself whom, in today's Reading, Jesus promises his followers, and whose first gifts to those who receive him are 'love, joy and peace' (cf. Gal 5:22).

Sixth Week
Monday
John 15:26-16:4

The disciples of Jesus (and we are among them) are to be witnesses to Jesus in a hostile world, a world which is hostile to Jesus' followers precisely because they continue, in every age, to keep Jesus present to the sight and hearing of a world which was first hostile to him (cf. 5th Wk, Sat.). Sharing Jesus' truth, Jesus' followers share in the 'so great opposition from sinners' (cf. Heb 12:3) which he endured. The trials attendant on their mission of witness are the passion of Jesus in them.

Jesus warns them at this solemn moment — perhaps lest they should think that, after his resurrection, they would be living in an era of messianic peace and tranquility. He had also warned them previously (cf. Mt 10:17-20) about magistrates and governors and kings; now he includes persecution by religious powers (cf. Lk 12:11-12). There will be people like Paul, who later confessed, 'I once thought it my duty to use every means to oppose the name of Jesus ...' (cf. Acts 26:9-11).

However, the witnesses to Jesus are never alone. The Spirit of Jesus will be in them; and it is the witness which the Spirit bears to Jesus (v. 26) that the disciples themselves bear. Thus Stephen's opponents found that they could not get the better of him 'because it was the Spirit that prompted what he said' (cf. Acts 6:9-10).

Because Jesus has made us, also, his witnesses, we, too, can confidently rely on the Spirit's guidance, his counsel, and his power. Come, Holy Spirit!

Sixth Week
Tuesday
John 16:5-11

Continuing on from yesterday's Reading, today's goes on to say that the world's attitude to the witnesses to Jesus (as its attitude to Jesus himself) reveals its attitude, ultimately, to God its Creator. The world wishes to organise itself without reference to God, and will oppose anyone or any institution that insists not only that God must be taken into account but also that God must be accounted to.

Whether the world acknowledges it or not, judgement is being passed on it. Jesus had already told Nicodemus that judgement was being passed on the world because it preferred darkness to the Light (cf. Jn 3:19), preferred blindness to sight (cf. Jn 9:39). He had already said that in crucifying him, the world was condemning itself (cf. Jn 12:31).

It is a task of the Holy Spirit to prove the world wrong in its sin (that is, in its refusal to believe in Jesus: v. 9); in its obstinate self-righteousness which (unlike the true righteousness of Jesus which is vindicated in his resurrection and ascension) does not lead to the Father (v. 10); and in its crucifixion of Jesus — that saving event which broke the power of the Prince of this world (v. 11).

What the Holy Spirit does in regard to the world he works, also, in the human heart: he moves us to acknowledge that we are sinners, and that, of ourselves, we have no righteousness, of ourselves can not be right before God; but he also convinces us that we find salvation in the crucifixion of Jesus who, dying, destroyed our death and, rising, restored our life.

Sixth Week
Wednesday
John 16:12-15

To each of us, also, Jesus has 'many things to say' (v. 12) — but not now, not all at once. But if we are docile to the Spirit whom he has sent to us to abide in us and to guide us, we shall, as our lives unfold, be always doing the will of him who has sent us, in our own time and place, as witnesses to him who always, as he himself said, did the will of the One who sent him (cf. Jn 8:29).

And as Jesus says in that same place, 'He who sent me is with me, and has not left me to myself', so Jesus, through his Spirit, is always with us whom he in turn has sent, never leaving us to ourselves. For, as Cardinal Newman says, 'Left to ourselves we should always take the wrong way; we must leave it to him' — to him who acts in us through his Spirit who has been poured abroad in our hearts.

Jesus, therefore, gives us his own Spirit; and everything the Spirit tells us is what Jesus himself would tell us (v. 13) — just as everything that Jesus told us is what he had heard from the Father who is the source of life. And this he used as a proof that we were regarded by him not as servants but as friends: 'I call you friends because I have made known to you everything I have heard from my Father' (cf. Jn 15:15).

We, in turn, are true 'friends' to the world about us if, by our lives, we silently tell them what we ourselves, through faith, have heard.

Sixth Week
Thursday (when not the Ascension)
John 16:16-20

The themes of loving one another, the hatred of the world, and Jesus' injunction to us to remember that the servant is not greater than the master have recurred frequently in the course of the Gospel Readings in recent days: and we might do well to return to them again today.

Or we might prefer to take for our prayer one point from today's Reading — Jesus' choice of us.

Today's brief Reading makes three points regarding Jesus' choice of us. First, it is he who has chosen us — not we who have chosen him (v. 16). Next, he has chosen us for a purpose — to commission us to go out into the world of our own time and place, and to be active in it on his behalf — that is, by giving it the words of him who alone has the words of eternal life (cf. Jn 6:63, 68). Thirdly, his choice of us has so withdrawn us from the world that we do not belong to the world (v. 19) — within which, nevertheless, and for which, we must spend (in both senses) our lives. (The 'world', we remember, is the refusal to believe in Jesus; it is the desire of human society to organise life without reference to God.)

Jesus sends us into a minefield — or, as he said, as sheep among wolves (cf. Mt 10:16). But we obey his command confidently: for not only in our ears rings the word 'Go!', but also his words, 'Be brave! I have conquered the world' (cf. Jn 16:33). And we go, not left to ourselves, but in the strength of him in whom we can do all things (cf. Phil 4:13).

The Ascension of the Lord
Years A, B, C

Not only the word pictures of the Scriptures (e.g. Lk 24:50-53, Acts 1:6-11) but also great paintings by great artists make it easy for us to create our own mental picture of the scene we are contemplating today. We are there to hear Jesus' oft-repeated, now final, promise of the Spirit, and to hear his oft-given, now

75

finally given, commission to go out into the world of our own place and time and bear witness to him.

We are there to see him withdraw himself from us and a cloud receive him out of our sight, as we strain to catch one last glimpse of him. But only our hearts can go up with him — rejoicing, nevertheless; for as he said, 'If you loved me, you would be glad to know that I am going to the Father (cf. Jn 14:28).

St Leo the Great points out that we rejoice, also, because, in Christ, our lowly human nature was raised beyond the height of all the powers of heaven to the throne of God the Father; for, as St Augustine says, since he is our Head and we are his Body so we, too, are already with him in heaven — not yet in physical reality but in the sure and certain hope of the resurrection.

A third cause for rejoicing is this (again in St Augustine's words) that as he did not leave heaven when he came down to us from heaven (being one with the Father always) so he did not leave us when he ascended to heaven again. He had promised: '*Know* that I am with you always' (cf. Mt 28:20); and again, 'Where two or three are gathered in my name, I shall be there among them' (cf. Mt 18:20).

Together with the disciples we hear the angels' words; and the meaning of them is, surely, that henceforth we are to witness not only to his resurrection but also to his abiding presence among us, and that it is through the joyousness of our hearts that we will most bear that witness.

The three-fold gladness which fills our thoughts today is not meant only for our own comforting; it should also spur us on to proclaim the Good News to others, so that all may have and experience this same joy in the Lord who is ever present to us.

So here we are: already seated with Christ in glory, and yet on earth as witnesses to his abiding presence among mankind — a witness most effectively given if we do as St Paul says:

'If you have risen with Christ, seek the things that are above where Christ is ...' (cf. Col 3:1-4).

Sixth Week
Friday
John 16:20-23

Birth pangs and the joy of beholding a new-born child (v. 21) ... Good Friday followed by Easter Sunday ... The trials of this life consummated in the glory that will be revealed in us (cf. Rom 8:18) ... Sorrow for a time swallowed up in perfect and imperishable joy (v. 22) ... Manifold puzzlement resolved in total enlightenment (v. 23) ... A time for asking satisfied in fully receiving (v. 23): and all this is, and only in, the name of Jesus (v. 21) — that is to say, through and because of Jesus' life, death, and resurrection.

These are the all-encompassing things which today's Reading, for all its brevity, puts before us.

Without Jesus there is no future, no final and immutable consummation of all that is transitory, changeable, incomplete, questioned but unanswered (because, without Jesus, unanswerable) about this life.

What the return of Jesus to his disciples in his resurrection (their seeing him again: v. 22) did for them, what the death of the faithful followers of Jesus does for them, are images (still partly constricted by their being framed in time and place) of the unconfined realities of Jesus' final Return and the definitive Coming of his Kingdom.

But those images are themselves supportive, heartening: for they themselves exist only because of the greater final reality to which they point, of which they are a tangible assurance, of which they partake.

'In joyful hope, we look forward ...'

Sixth Week
Saturday
John 16:23-28

How plainly, now, Jesus speaks:
I came from the Father
and have come into the world,
and now I leave the world
to go to the Father (v. 28).

The cycle is complete: the purpose of the Son's becoming man and dwelling among us is fulfilled. The disciples are not to regard Jesus' crucifixion and death as 'a disaster', his leaving them 'like annihilation' (cf. Wis 3:1). On the contrary, it is his glorification and the world's salvation.

But, as for Jesus, so also for his followers: the way to the Father is through the terrible reality of the cross.

Through the cross, Jesus opens up for his disciples and for us the way to the Father — for by our faith in and love of Jesus we are made one with him and thereby become the receivers of the Father's love. Through his resurrection, Jesus becomes our Mediator, ever living to make intercession for us (cf. Heb 7:25); it is, therefore appropriate now that we petition the Father in his name (v. 26) — even while we are so closely identified with him that it is as if our prayer were his prayer, and he had no need to ask on our behalf (v. 26).

The hour that Jesus said was coming (v. 25) has come: we live in an age that has been ushered in by the resurrection of Jesus and the coming of the Holy Spirit. Because of the enlightenment it brings regarding our relationship with Jesus and, through him, with the Father, it is an age of joy (v. 24).

Christians, St Paul says, are people who rejoice in hope, who rejoice in their sufferings, who rejoice in God (cf. Rom 5:1-11).

Seventh Week of Easter

Seventh Sunday of Easter

The gospel Readings for this the last Sunday before Pentecost divide among themselves 'The Priestly Prayer of Christ' (Jn 17:1-26) which follows Jesus' final discourse to the·disciples at the Last Supper.

Following this Prayer, John resumes his narrative with (18:1), 'After he had said all this, Jesus went out with his disciples' — into the night, and into the garden of Gethsemane, there to enter into his agony.

Seventh Sunday
Year A
John 17:1-11

There are many references in the gospels to Jesus at prayer — prayer which, often, was quite prolonged; but today's Reading gives us the only example we have of the contents of Jesus' longer prayer. Since prayer of the kind recorded here is a very personal thing, it is unlikely that this chapter of John's gospel intends to teach us how to pray — at least not in the sense in which 'the words our Saviour gave us', in response to his disciples' request, are clearly set before us as a model.

Nevertheless, we are able, indirectly, to pick up a few hints as to what is always valid for our own prayer. 'Jesus raised his eyes to heaven' (v. 1) — a gesture common in the prayer tradition in which he himself was brought up. It reminds us that when we pray we do so as human beings, not as disembodied spirits, and that, consequently, even the positions we adopt, any gesture we make at time of prayer (unless they are thoughtlessly mechanical) are of importance. St Ignatius, for example, says that one ought embark on prayer kneeling, prostrate, supine, sitting, standing — whatever is most helpful to one's concentration on the matter in hand.

So, too, each of the various postures we adopt in celebrating the Liturgy has its own particular connotation in order to create in us a succession of attitudes of mind and heart — joy, attentive listening, reverence, and so on. We must guard against their becoming mere routine.

Jesus begins his prayer with the word, 'Father': he is praying out of the intimacy of the relationship of his Sonship of the Father. St Ignatius also suggests that, according to what we want to pray about, we picture ourselves in some particular guise or condition: a recreant knight before his King, a guilty wretch before the supreme Judge, a servant talking to his Master, a friend talking to a Friend. And, of course, Jesus himself taught us to address his Father as our Father.

Thus, in the first half of today's Reading (vs. 1-5) Jesus prays out of the relationship of Son-to-Father. In the second half (vs. 6-11a) he prays out of his relationship to his disciples.

As Son, Jesus has been given power over all creation (v. 2) — an authority of which he will remind his followers (after his resurrection) to encourage them in their missionary activity (cf. Mt 28:18). But he is given this authority not for his own or for its sake but in order to give eternal life to all (v. 2). This is the true purpose of all authority, and the true exercise of authority consists in the service of others, not in self-glori-fication or self-aggrandisement. Prayer for those in authority (temporal or spiritual) and the proper use of any authority we might have are an important part of our christian calling.

As Son, Jesus has glorified the Father by finishing the work his Father had given him to do (v. 4) — that is, to accomplish the work of salvation of the human race through the willing acceptance of his death on the cross — hanging on which his last words are, 'It is accomplished' (Jn 19:30).

As children of the Father, we, too, are given a work to do — to make known his name to those whose lives impinge on ours (v. 6) and to give glory to God by the visible fulfilment of his will in our lives.

Seventh Sunday
Year B
John 17:11-19

Jesus is on the threshold of his departure from this world back to the Father from whom he had come into the world — and had come precisely in order to make the Father known. But his disciples are to remain behind. After his resurrection, he will assure them that he is with them always, even to the end of time (cf. Mt 28:20). But from their point of view, he will then have gone. And so, solicitous for them, he prays for them — praying for them out of the situation which will be theirs: he no longer visibly with them to keep them (v. 12), and they in a world hostile to them because they do not belong to it (vs. 14-15).

Not directly but by implication, this prayer of Jesus for his disciples (whom he is leaving but whom he will not leave orphans: cf. Jn 14:18) deals with the perennial relationship of the Church (and the individual follower of Jesus in every age) to the world — the world being named eight times in six verses.

Jesus points to the Father as the model of this relationship. For the one and only time in this gospel, Jesus addresses the Father as 'Holy Father' — 'holy' being the word traditionally used to signify God's 'apartness' from the world.

The 'world' from which God is 'apart', and from which the followers of Jesus must be 'apart', is not, of course, the material creation, for it is not only good in itself but also serves to draw human beings to know the Creator of it (cf. Wis 13:1-9; Rom 2:20). Nor, in this context, is the world the world of human affairs.

The 'world' in which we must have no part, as God has no part in it, is the non-acceptance of Jesus (cf. Jn 1:11); it is the darkness which opposes the light (cf. Jn 3:19-20); it is the evil which persecutes goodness (v. 14) — and it is embodied in people.

Yet even this world is so loved by God that 'he gave his only Son . . . so that the world might be saved' (cf. Jn 3:14-18) when that same Son gave his life as a ransom for all (cf. Mk 10:45). 'What proves God's love for us,' St Paul writes, 'is that Christ died for us while we were still sinners' (Rom 5:8).

These two poles create the tension in which the Church and every follower of Christ must live. Jesus' disciples cannot be removed from the world (v. 14) for their mission is to that world. They cannot, therefore, escape that world's hatred and persecution (cf. Jn 15:17-21). What they must do is not model themselves on the behaviour of the world around them (cf. Rom 12:2), for to make the world their friend is to make God their enemy (cf. Jas 4:4) since 'The love of the Father cannot be in anyone who loves the world' (1 Jn 2:15). And yet they must love the world even to the point of dying for its salvation as Jesus did and could, therefore, say, 'I have overcome the world' (Jn 16:33) — not by condemning it but by redeeming it.

Hence Jesus prays that the Father would 'consecrate them in the truth' — that is to say, would equip them for their mission through the firmness of their faith. As John writes (1 Jn 5:4): 'This is the victory over the world — our faith'; for it is only through faith, and the love it inspires, that we can be not overcome by evil but overcome evil with good (cf. Rom 12:21).

Seventh Sunday
Year C
John 17:20-26

With today's Reading, Jesus brings to an end the great Priestly Prayer which, in John's gospel, he utters on the night in which he was betrayed. In its first phase (Year A) he prays out of his unique relationship of Son-to-Father. In its second phase (Year B) he prays out of his relationship to his disciples. In today's final phase, he prays out of the relationship of his immediate disciples to future believers — us ourselves; for he says, 'I pray not only for these, but also for those who, through their words, will believe in me' (v. 20).

It is very moving to reflect upon, seeing them in the mind's eye, the vast number of faithful witnesses to Jesus — some great, some small; some heroic, some, perhaps, faint-hearted — through whom we ourselves are linked to the scene we contemplate in today's Reading. So to reflect is also a spur to us to take our place in that chain so that by the witness of our lives, if not through our words, others will come to believe in Jesus, or be strengthened in their faith in him.

What Jesus asks of his Father for his immediate disciples he asks, also, for us: that we may all be one in heart and mind (v. 22) in this life and, in the next, come to be with him forever (cf. 1 Thess 4:17) and to see his glory through which we ourselves shall be glorified (v. 24) — just as, in this life, we have received of his own fulness of grace (cf. Jn 1:16).

He prays, also, that we may be absorbed into the mystery of Trinitarian love when the love with which the Father loves him may be in us and that he may be in us (v. 26) so that he may find a dwelling-place in our hearts, so that our lives are grounded in love and founded on love, and we come to know the breadth and length and height and depth of the love of Jesus which surpasses all knowing (cf. Eph 3:17-19).

And this is why we so look forward to next Sunday and the coming of the Holy Spirit, for it is through the Spirit's being given to us that the love of God is poured abroad in our hearts (cf. Rom 5:5).

'The Father and I are one,' says Jesus (Jn 10:30); and this oneness between Father and Son is the source and model of every relationship between Jesus and his disciples, and between his followers in relation to one another.

Is it a question of mission? 'As the Father has sent me, so also I send you' (Jn 20:21). A question of mutual love? 'As the Father has loved me, so have I loved you; love one another as I have loved you' (Jn 15:9, 12). A question of unity? 'With me in them and you in me, may they be completely one' (v. 21).

The conclusion of v. 23 puts unity on an equal footing with love, as far as the signs of discipleship of Jesus are concerned. 'By this love you have for one another, everyone will know that you are my disciples' (Jn 13:35); while here the disciples' unity is the sign to the world that Jesus was sent by the Father.

Hence, when St Paul begs us to live a life worthy of our Christian calling, he writes; 'Bear with one another charitably, in complete selflessness, gentleness and patience. Do all you can to preserve the unity of the Spirit by the peace that binds you together' (cf. Eph 4:1-6).

Seventh Week
Monday
John 16:29-33

The disciples respond to the crystal-clear statement Jesus has just made (the conclusion to the Reading of last Saturday); but their response (vs. 29-30) is both precipitate and only partial in its commitment. They are laying claim to a kind of faith which is possible only with the resurrection of Jesus and the enlightenment of the Holy Spirit. Peter's earlier confession, 'You are the Christ . . .' (cf. Mt 16:16) was, Jesus said, a response to a revelation of the Father. But here it is simply a conviction the disciples have reached — that Jesus has come from God. This expression of belief stops far short of what Jesus has just said. It is as if they have not understood, let alone believed, Jesus' statement that he is leaving the world to go to the Father.

Jesus tells them clearly how far that faith of theirs will carry them: they will be scattered in dismay when they see him hand himself over to his enemies (cf. Mt 26:56). So he had already warned them: 'You will all lose faith in me this night . . .' (cf. Mt 26:30). But Jesus truly loves his disciples.

At his arrest in Gethsemane, he will ensure their safety (cf. Jn 18:8); so now he tells them not to despair when they realise their desertion of him, but to find peace again in him (v. 33).

And this is still Jesus' attitude to all his followers in their falls and their weakness.

That reassurance which Jesus gives them the disciples will need in the hours immediately ahead of them. In the years to come, too, they will need reassurance in the difficulties they will encounter. That reassurance is given in the resurrection which proclaims the truth of Jesus' words: 'I have overcome the world' (v. 33).

And through him and with him and in him we, too, are conquerors (cf. Rom 8:35-39).

Seventh Week
Tuesday
John 17:1-11

The Gospel Reading for today is that of the 7th Sunday, Year A.

Seventh Week
Wednesday
John 17:11-19

The Gospel Reading for today is that of the 7th Sunday, Year B.

Seventh Week
Thursday
John 17:20-26

The Gospel Reading for today is that of the 7th Sunday, Year C.

Seventh Week
Friday
John 21:15-19

Today's and tomorrow's Readings bring to a close the Good News according to John. Both Readings come from what seems to be an Appendix to the body of that Gospel; and the incidents they put before us occur in the lovely surroundings we have contemplated and the unique atmosphere we have breathed when the first half of this chapter was our appointed Reading (cf. 3rd Sunday, Year C).

The liturgical use of this incident is powerful. Today and tomorrow we, so to speak, see Jesus standing among us for the last time. Henceforth, it is through his Spirit (whose pentecostal coming is imminent) that he will be among us and with us until the end of time.

Today, Jesus pressingly questions Peter regarding the apostle's love for him (vs. 15-17). In part, the three-fold questioning rehabilitates Peter after his three-fold denial of Jesus at the time of the passion. But it is more: it is also a solemn commissioning of Peter in his pastoral office (vs. 15-17), and, also, a repetition of the call, 'Follow me' (v. 19).

To all who protest their love for him, Jesus will give these same two things: a task to perform, and an offer of an intimate relationship.

The Jesus who issues that summons is the crucified and risen Jesus; and he tells Peter quite bluntly that he is being called to share in that crucifixion and so give glory to God (v. 9) — just as Jesus' own crucifixion was his own being glorified and his supreme act of giving glory to God through his 'becoming obedient even to accepting death on the cross' (cf. Phil 2:8).

And what Jesus says to Peter he says also to his Church — and to each of his followers individually.

Seventh Week
Saturday
John 21:20-25

It would seem that after Jesus had spoken to Peter they began to take a stroll together, and John started off to join them (v. 20). Peter notices John and, perhaps recalling how different from his own was John's behaviour at the time of Jesus' passion, he wonders (even while still digesting what Jesus had just foretold regarding his own destiny) what will be John's fate. Impulsive as ever, Peter immediately voices his thought (v. 21).

Jesus answers Peter's question by refusing an answer. According to Jesus' reply, what matters is not what becomes of John (even a fanciful living until Jesus comes again) but that Jesus' will be fulfilled in his disciple.

So it is with every follower of Jesus. The essential thing is to do the will of Jesus. This, of course, means that it has to be recognised that the concrete circumstances in which the will of Jesus is done will be different for different people. Thus (as is often pointed out) in today's scene Peter is called to be a shepherd, John is called to be a witness; but each is equally called to do the will of Jesus.

This, in John's gospel, is Jesus' last word on what it means to be a disciple of his. So often Jesus speaks of himself as doing the will of his Father and of speaking and acting only as his Father would have him speak and act.

Here, in his final word, Jesus intimates that discipleship of him is to be modelled on his sonship of the Father.

Pentecost

Pentecost Sunday

With the coming of the Holy Spirit, the first Gift of the risen Lord to his Church, the Easter Season comes to its end — in a new beginning.

Although alternative gospel Readings are provided for each of the three Years, it is normally that of Year A which is read — those given for Years B and C being purely optional. Moreover, the event which today's Liturgy celebrates is found in the First Reading — Acts 2:1-11; and it is with the event itself that today's Reflection is naturally concerned.

Pentecost
Years A, B, C

Today's celebration of the coming of the Holy Spirit, the first Gift of the risen Jesus to his Church, brings the Easter Season to its end. For now the purpose of Jesus' coming into our world is completed — the Father has been made known, and has been glorified through the obedience of the Son; mankind has been redeemed, and the two-fold resurrection (from estrangement from God to oneness with him, and from mortality to immortality) has been proclaimed; the Church which will carry Christ's name and his Good News to the ends of the earth and to the end of time is now fully constituted, and is henceforth indwelt by the Spirit as Animator, Guide and Consoler.

The event which we celebrate today reproduces in the Church the reality which was accomplished in Jesus' own person at his baptism by John. On that occasion Jesus was proclaimed to be the Father's Son, sent by him for all to hear, and was anointed for his mission by the Holy Spirit. The mysteries of that event in the life of Jesus are today reproduced in the Church, which is the Body of Christ. The Church is today inaugurated as Witness to Jesus, and is anointed for that mission of witness by the outpouring of the Holy Spirit.

The gospel writers tell us that immediately after his baptism Jesus was led by the Spirit (Mark very forcefully says, 'the Spirit drove him') into the wilderness, there to be put to the test by Satan. Henceforth, Jesus is led by the Spirit. It is by the Holy Spirit that he cast out the powers of evil (cf. Mt 12:28), that he spoke in the synagogue at Nazareth (cf. Lk 4:14-18), that he chose his Apostles (cf. Acts 1:2).

Throughout the Easter Season, in our reading of the *Acts of the Apostles,* we have seen that the same is true of the post-pentecostal Church. The activity of the Spirit is named every-where, making the Apostles bold to proclaim the risen Jesus, and directing their missionary activity.

93

What is true of Jesus himself, what is true of the Church which is the Body of Christ, should also be true of ourselves. 'They who are children of God,' says St Paul, 'are led by the Spirit of God' (cf. Rom 8:14); and, of the role of the Holy Spirit in our lives, he writes, 'If the Spirit is the source of our life, let the Spirit also direct the course of our life' (cf. Gal 5:25).

The Christian's 'spiritual life' is precisely that — 'spiritual'; that is to say, a life lived in the Spirit who has made his home in us (cf. Rom 8:9), in whom all of us have been washed clean (cf. 1 Cor 6:11) and of whom all of us have drunk (cf. 1 Cor 12:13). It is this Holy Spirit, living in us and in whom we live, who enables us to call God our Father (cf. Rom 8:15), to proclaim 'Jesus is Lord' (cf. 1 Cor 12:3) to put an end to the misdeeds of the body (cf. Rom 8:13). It is the Holy Spirit who enables us to understand the wisdom of God (cf. 1 Cor 2:10), who supports us in our weakness and who, when we do not know what to say, himself prays for us (cf. Rom 8:26).

'By their fruits you shall know them,' says Jesus. When we are trying to live as children of God, led by the Spirit of God, we must work to bring forth, make visible and operative in our lives those fruits of the Holy Spirit of which St Paul writes (in Gal 5:22): joy, peace, patience, kindness, goodness, long-suffering, gentleness, faith, modesty, self-control, chastity.